Talk with yourself

Meditative Texts and Illustrations

Renate Younis

Talk with yourself

Meditative Texts und Illustrations

Bibliographic information of the Deutsche Nationalbibliothek:

The German National Library records this publication in the German national bibliography;
detailed bibliographic data are available on the Internet
http://dnb.dnb.de

Translation from German Gabriele Neumann/ London

Production & Publishing:
BoD - Books on Demand, Norderstedt

ISBN: 9783746017914

Content

9   Author's Note

14   Give your Self time

16   Come into the silence that resides within you

18   Feel your body the way it is

20   Breathe consciously and deeply

22   Meet your inner being

24   Acknowledge your Self

26   Enter your inner cosmos

28   Envelop yourself with the highest vibration

30   Dive deep into yourself

32   Presence

34   Be in the divine moment

36   Endow your self confidence

38   You know that you know

40   More than your intuition

42   You never lost connection with yourself

44   Travel daily to your Self

46   Distractions

48   Your soul speaks only to you

50   Realise the difference

52   Go beyond your fears

54   Feel soul closeness

56   Understand soul language

58   Integrate your experiences

60   Your soul fills you

62	Soul realisation
64	You experience to be a creator
66	You complement yourself
68	You allow transformations
70	You inform yourself
72	You are in charge of the conversation
74	Listen sensitively to your soul
76	Time without time
78	Is the human you are ready?
80	Feel appreciation for yourself
82	Breathe, breathe

8

Author's Note

For a long time we have been listening to external voices, to the voices of parents, teachers and friends, but also to the voices of angels when we needed answers. This is how we learned. We accepted these limitations. These familiar voices are outside and above you. It's just an old habit that we follow. We are constantly sharing information with other people in social networks. However, we don't enter the interior space within, to meet ourselves. It's not a space we step into naturally or we avoid it unconsciously.

Like me, do you feel that it is time to grow out of this discomfort? Do you want to be with yourself and to create a natural sense of well-being?

Are you ready to pause and expand your communication with yourself? Are you longing to really pay attention to yourself now, and to dissolve the separation from your Self?

You can talk on many different levels to yourself. For example, you can ask your body a question or you can immerse into your essence, wordlessly, as a time of Self Love.

You can naturally ask yourself for advice, support and help. You can ask yourself, "What is really important for me right now?"

At the same time, you are opening yourself to information and impulses of your inner wisdom that will support you. You gain access to your inner strength.

You don't withdraw from the world. When you are connected to your inner world, you can truly express yourself in your environment. You come to a new balance with yourself and with other people.

Initially, the contact with your Self will be diffuse, a bit indistinct. But over time, as you get to know each other better, you will become more proficient in understanding your living soul.

Dialoguing with yourself is a quiet step that you can take in your own sovereignty and independence.

Your eternal, loving inner being is already waiting to hear your human concerns. It would like to take part in your life as a human being and no longer be separated from it.

Over time, you become safer and more familiar during your inner dialogues with yourself. Expect surprises and of course new things in your life, especially more fulfilment.

The colour-intensive illustrations in acrylic are from my series "Planets of Change", which always produced new wisdom pearls. They support you with their vibration when you open yourself to the path to your inner being. Likewise, the variety and depth of your personal contact with yourself is stimulated.

I wish you much joy in your communication within your visible and invisible worlds, but above all in the fulfilling dialogue experience with your true Self.

Renate Younis

Hamburg, November 2017

Take a few deep breaths ...

Give your Self time

Make yourself comfortable while lying or sitting down. Make sure that you will be undisturbed for some time for your inner conversation. Close your eyes. This is a time for you alone. This is your special time.

15

Come into the silence that resides within in you

You can only hear your inner voice when you get calm yourself. Your inner being is often very quiet in its expression and is often not perceived in its tenderness. Take the time you need to find your way into your silence.

17

Feel your body as it is

First, turn your awareness to your body. You can first perceive and feel your body as a whole. You can also direct your attention to your body. Just observe, without wanting to change anything. Your judgment-free affection pleases your physical body, especially when it's tense and hardened.

Breathe consciously and deeply

Your breath carries you from moment to moment. Let your breaths flow naturally as you follow them like an observer. By itself, your breath becomes deeper and more even. Your breath is your stream of life that moves through your physicality, which rocks, nourishes, and at the same time permeates you. You can expand into your breath and advance into deeper areas within you.

21

Meet your inner being

Watch how your thoughts are constantly active. Look from the outside onto these lines of thoughts, without refusing or preferring anything. How are you feeling right now?

Let all emotions be there as it is. Allow yourself the attention of feeling yourself. Enjoy your inner wealth in your body, which is constantly changing.

Acknowledge your Self

You are more than an imperfect human being; you are more than your personality. You are a child of this Earth with a spiritual origin.

Your soul exists forever. You are here to undergo experiences as a human being, inner and outer.

Always, your very personally-felt experiences make up your sense of being.

Enter your inner cosmos

When you turn inward, you encounter your infinite inner world. Your potentials are unlimited. Your inner dialogue with yourself begins by seeing with your inner eyes, listening with your inner ears and feeling inward.

Here in your inner world your inner wisdom resides. The inner answers to your questions are already here.

27

Envelop your Self with the highest vibration

When you go deep inside, you encounter a loving energy. That's the love you carry inside of you. You are invited to be carried by your own love, to be guided by it. It fulfils an ancient dream of you, you give yourself love. Now!

29

Dive deep into your Self

Completely let go of all your perceptions, so that you find yourself inhabiting space where words can no longer be found. You go beyond relaxation and peace. You are only awareness and breath. You are a free, weightless being in nothingness.

31

Presence

In openly feeling and listening into the presence beyond your mind, in the perception of your perception, in complete bodily presence you are wide awake and receiving what now wants to come to you.

Be in the divine moment

You can't hear your soul? Stay in the divine moment of NOW. Let go of what was in the past and what will be in the future. In the present moment that receives your undivided attention, your soul voice steps forward.

35

Give your Self confidence

Your inner Soul Self wants to take care of you. Trust the impulses that you receive in your inner conversations. Everything is appropriate and won't overwhelm you. The inner impulses that come from your inner wisdom help you to take steps of fulfilment in your life.

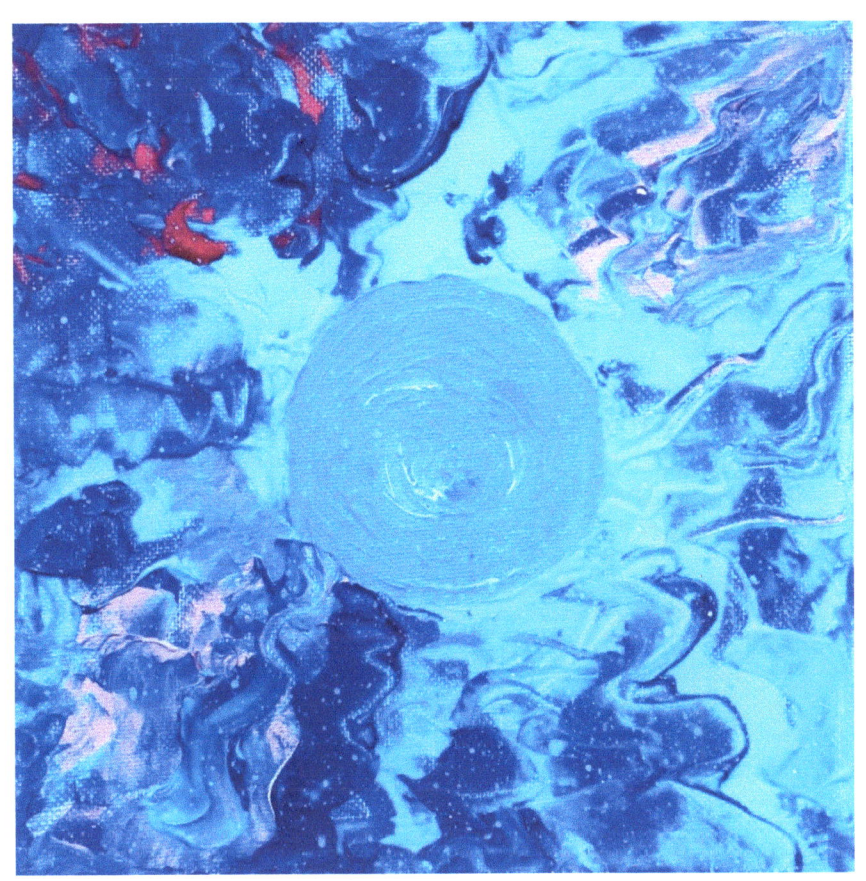

You know that you know

Even if you feel emptiness within you, you give yourself an answer. Don't try to grasp this with the mind. Allow yourself to be in compassion and deep peace with yourself. You are always at the right time, in the right place. Everything that is, serves you in a perfect and graceful way.

39

More than your intuition

Your intuitive knowledge, dreams and gut instincts have often helped you. Now expand yourself, into your divine consciousness, what you are and always will be. Feel yourself in your essence with your very own unique vibration.

41

You never lost connection with your Self

You just forgot to contact your Self. You have put more faith in others than in your Self. You can rediscover your Self. The connection to your Self transforms everything. Feel your Self while allowing yourself all feelings. You have come to life.

Travel daily to your Self

Nurture the connection to your inner Self daily so that a relationship with your Self can develop. These can be short, intense sequences in everyday life, as well as a deliberately chosen time that you spend with yourself. Get out of the need to make an effort or achieve something. Open up in your communication with your Self with ease. Your soul is always listening to you.

45

Distractions

There are a lot of interesting Distractions that you will encounter. These are topics that get your attention and keep you busy. There are other people who have something to say. It's your troubled, doubting aspects that don't want to look inward. Recognize them, breathe and come back to your silent core.

47

Your soul speaks only to you

Your soul shows itself to you in a special and unique way. Only you are important to your soul. Only you can receive, understand and integrate the messages of your soul. Let your soul be near you again.

49

Realise the difference

Not every impulse you receive comes from your soul. There are layers of mass consciousness, of other people's thinking, and of your mind. The message of your inner wisdom will always feel warm and loving. Use your feelings as a guide.

51

Go beyond your fears

Be aware of your perceptions and feelings while in contact with your Self. Allow yourself to enter unchartered territory. You walk on unknown paths that aren't traversed yet. Your breaths will carry you, even if you meet fears. These fears have been hiding in secrecy. Now they can move on and dissolve.

53

Feel soul closeness

When you really feel your own soul for the first time, you gift yourself with an unforgettable experience that touches you in the depths of your heart.

The love of your soul can be overwhelming, so close and so familiar. Your home is coming directly to you.

Understand soul language

Your soul can express itself in many different ways. It is not limited to human words that can be silent or very clear. Your soul gives you impulses for action, colour, light or scent-information that you can't grasp with the thinking mind.

Integrate your experiences

Accept your experiences of communicating with yourself and integrate them into your everyday life. Allow yourself to perceive internal resistance or defense. Allow yourself to grow beyond that.

Your soul satisfies you

When you come in contact with your soul, you notice a deep satisfaction. You nourish yourself at all levels of your existence through your own soul nectar. The restless, hungry search for answers outside of you ceases.

61

Soul realisation

The linear separation in you transforms into a sweeping circle of yourself and your soul, with no beginning or end. This is done by you. It is an act of perfect grace that you can't imagine. It's a change of direction that makes you whole.

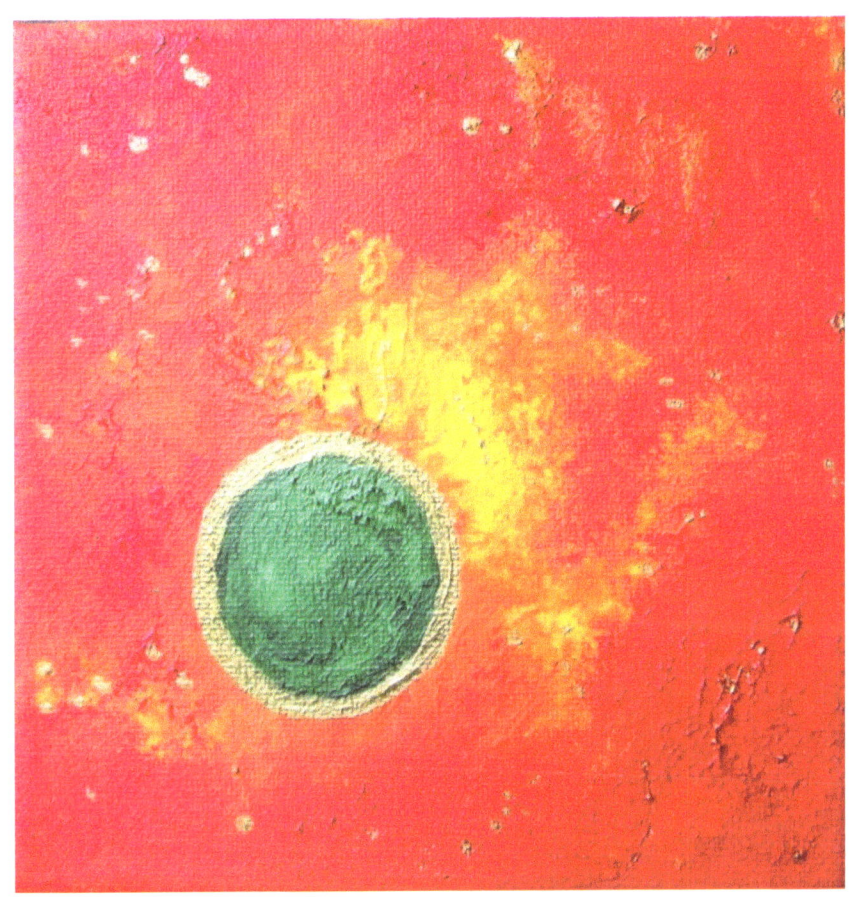

63

You experience to be a creator

In the communicative fusion between your human and divine nature, you experience your true essence. You completely change your concept of your Self, of your being. You are the creative manifestor of your life. Your inner and outer Self soulfully dance together.

You complement your Self

In returning home to your Self fully, in all dimensions you find healing and deep peace. You hold your Self and are held in the midst of your physical existence in all its facets. You don't avoid your Self anymore.

You allow transformation

You like spending time with your Self. Feeling your Self and breathing along as one with everything, you are completely with your Self. You go through a profound transformation as your home can come to you after a long, long time.

You inform your Self

Clarity and transparency are important in your new self-determination. So tell your Self what's currently happening and what you would like to happen! Share everything that moves you with your Self.

71

You are in charge of the conversation

Even if you feel distracted or self-sabotaged, losing the thread altogether, or just holding a thin thread in your hands, you can always create a new fabric for your Self with your conscious decision.

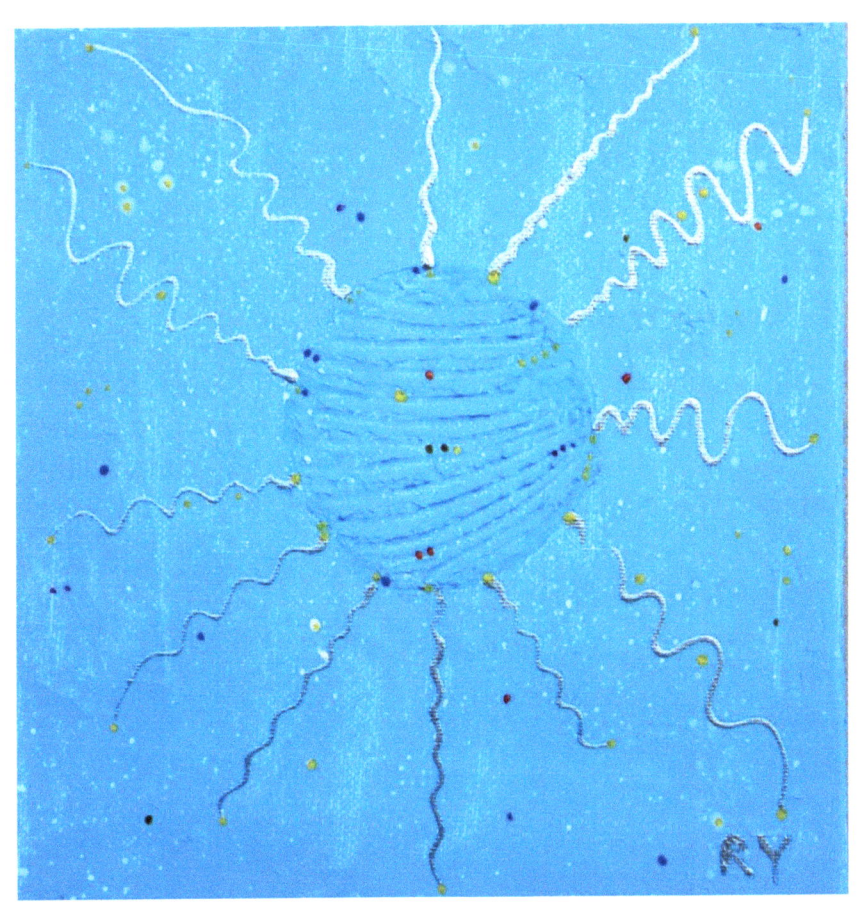

73

Listen sensitively to your soul

Your soul has always been close to you, even if you couldn't feel it. When you release all effort, all attempts to achieve something, it is simply there: the voice of your Self that you can intuitively understand. There is no distance between you and you anymore.

Time without time

Let your answer arrive in timelessness. You don't need a time limit or other constraints that might tamper the answer with unbalanced energy. You can rest assured that you will always receive your answer in the right way at the right time.

77

Is the human you are ready?

Have you reached the point where you communicate in both directions? To speak to your inner and outer Self, to interact in visible and invisible spaces - these abilities can only be awakened by your willingness, your permission and your allowance.

Feel appreciation for your Self

Only you can honour and appreciate your Self for being, no matter what experiences you have created for yourself. In communication with your inner source, there are treasures ready for you to be retrieved. Thank yourself for being ready and being able to discover and accept them.

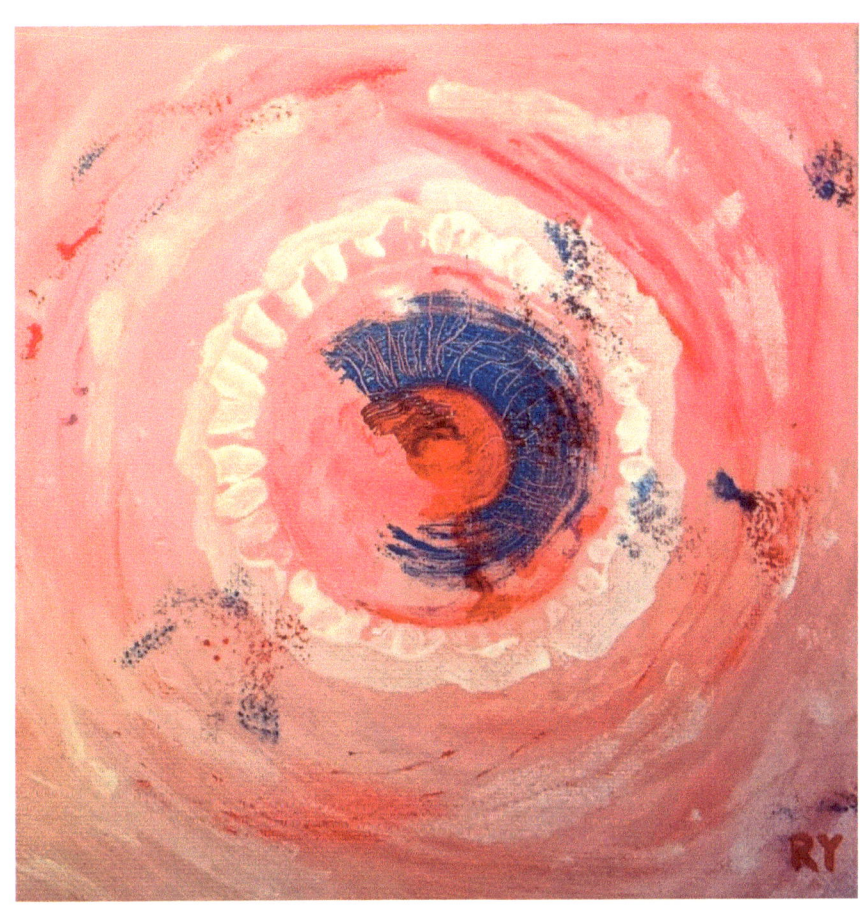

81

Breathe, breathe

Your conscious breaths allow you to easily and effectively move mental, emotional, and physical energies. Your breath is the bridge between your inner and outer Self. Breathe and follow your own inner invitation. You are always welcome just the way you are. Breathe and begin your inner dialogues.

83

Take some conscious breaths ...